Shaun the Sheep™

Save the Tree

LEVEL 3

Based on the TV series

Re-told by: Kathryn Harper
Series Editor: Melanie Williams

T0345781

Pearson Education Limited
Edinburgh Gate, Harlow,
Essex CM20 2JE, England
and Associated Companies throughout the world.

ISBN: 978-1-4479-3134-8

This edition first published by Pearson Education Ltd 2014
11
Text copyright © Pearson Education Ltd 2014

The moral rights of the author have been asserted
in accordance with the Copyright Designs and Patents Act 1988

Set in 17/21pt OT Fiendstar Regular
Printed in Great Britain by Bell and Bain Ltd, Glasgow
SWTC/02

Published by Pearson Education Ltd

For a complete list of the titles available in the Pearson English Kids Readers series, please go to
www.pearsonenglishkidsreaders.com. Alternatively, write to your local Pearson Education office or to
Pearson English Readers Marketing Department, Pearson Education, Edinburgh Gate, Harlow, Essex CM20 2JE, England.

It is a very cold morning on the farm. The fire is small. The farmer has to get more wood.

Brrrrrrr!

He is cold and he wants a big fire. This is not a good morning.

The farmer puts on his coat and hat. He wants to get some wood from the wood box.

He opens the box but there is no wood in it.
No wood! What can he do?

The farmer takes a long saw and his dog, Bitzer.
They have to go and cut down a tree.

They get into the old blue lorry and
drive down the road.

Rattle Rattle **Vroooom!**

Baaaaaaa!

The farmer is away. Now the sheep can play.

Hooray!

Shaun the Sheep and his friends go to their favourite tree. It is a big beautiful tree in the middle of the garden.

Some of the sheep jump into the tree and climb up it.
Other sheep play on the swings. Other sheep dance on
the grass and make music.

They are having a big party in the tree!

The farmer and Bitzer look and look but they cannot find a good tree for firewood.

These trees are small and thin. They are not good for a fire.

The farmer and Bitzer get into the lorry.

Vroooooom!

The farmer and Bitzer drive back to the house.

Rattle Rattle Vrooooom!

Up in the tree, Shaun sees the old blue lorry. It is coming down the road.

Baaa!

he says
to the other sheep.

The sheep hear Shaun. They stop playing, singing, jumping, climbing and swinging. Quickly, they leave the tree and walk on the grass.

The farmer and Bitzer arrive and the sheep are quietly eating grass.

Munch, munch, munch, baa, baaa, baaa ...

The farmer and Bitzer look at the big tree ... it is a good tree for firewood!

The farmer gets the saw.

Shaun sees the saw. Oh no! He and the other sheep have to save their favourite tree.

The farmer and Bitzer walk to the tree but three sheep are in front of them. They move again but the sheep move with them.

Now the farmer is very angry. He cannot get to the tree.

The farmer points to Bitzer. The dog puts three of the
sheep in the pen and closes the door after them. Some
other sheep try to stop the farmer but Bitzer puts them
in the pen.

The farmer and Bitzer are at the big tree. They take the saw and they are ready.

They do not look up. They do not see Shaun and the two big sheep in the tree.

Up in the tree, Shaun looks at the other two sheep and they look at him. They have to stop the farmer and Bitzer.

Ready?

NOW!

They jump down from the tree.

Shaun and the two sheep jump on the farmer.

Now the farmer is on the grass. Ow! What was that? Where did they come from?

He is under the sheep. He tries to move but the sheep are very heavy.

Bitzer is not happy. He puts the sheep in the pen. Now there are a lot of sheep in there.

Baaaaaaa!

The farmer is ready. The sheep are afraid but they cannot help the tree this time.

Baa, baaa, baaa ...

Suddenly, the farmer stops. He sees a happy face in the tree.

The farmer is surprised because he remembers that happy face from a long time ago ...

He was a boy! He carved that happy face!

The farmer was a small boy. He played under the tree, played on the swing and he climbed the tree. He loved the tree.

He was always happy near the tree because it was his favourite place.

The farmer carved the happy face into the tree because he loved the big tree. He was happier near the tree than at school or at home. It was his happy tree.

The farmer touches the happy face. He cannot cut the tree for firewood now because he loves it. It is his tree. He forgets about the saw and he hugs the tree.

AWWWWwwww ... his happy tree!

Now Bitzer is making beautiful music with the saw.

Shaun listens to it with the other sheep. They are happy because they saved the tree.

They can play in the tree for a long, long time.

Baaaa!

Activity page ❶

Before You Read

❶ Look at the cover. What kind of story do you think this is?

a   a funny story
b   a sad story
c   a true story
d   a boring story

❷ What do sheep usually do? Tick ✔.

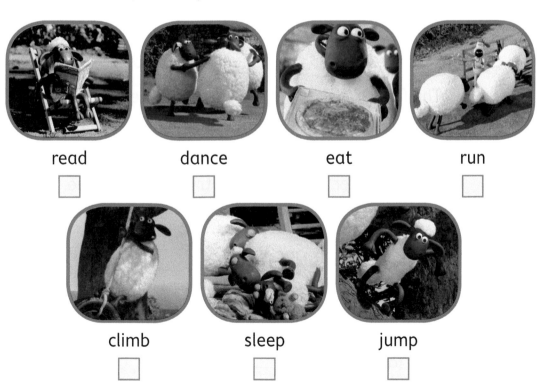

| read | dance | eat | run |
| ☐ | ☐ | ☐ | ☐ |

| climb | sleep | jump |
| ☐ | ☐ | ☐ |

Activity page ❷

After You Read

❶ Who does these things in the story?

a wants to cut down a tree
b hugs a tree
c plays in the tree
d plays a saw
e drives the lorry
f looks for firewood

 Bitzer  the farmer  Shaun the Sheep

❷ What happens first in the story?

a ☐ There is no wood.

☐ The sheep play in the tree.

b ☐ Shaun the Sheep sees the lorry.

☐ The trees are not good for firewood.

c ☐ The farmer sees the happy face.

☐ The farmer played on the swing.

d ☐ The sheep jump on the farmer.

☐ The farmer and Bitzer try to cut the tree.

❸ What do you think? Find the pages.

a This page is very funny. _____
b This page is a little sad. _____
c There are a lot of sheep on this page. _____
d This page is from many years ago. _____
e This is my favourite page. _____